THE UNSTORABLE BLESSING

Remove What Limits God's Ability To Pour Limitless Resources Through Your Life

David Wright

[19] *For the eyes of the LORD (search) throughout the earth to strengthen (show himself faithful to) <u>those whose hearts are fully committed to him</u>.*
    2 Chronicles 16:9a NIV (author's emphasis)

Copyright © 2024 David Wright

All rights reserved. No part of this book may be reproduced or used in any manner without written permission of the copyright owner except for the use of quotations in a book review.

All Scripture quotations, unless otherwise indicated, are taken from the Holy Bible, New International Version®, NIV®. Copyright ©1973, 1978, 1984, 2011 by Biblica, Inc.™ Used by permission of Zondervan. All rights reserved worldwide. www.zondervan.com. The "NIV" and "New International Version" are trademarks registered in the United States Patent and Trademark Office by Biblica, Inc.™ | Scripture taken from the New Century Version®. Copyright © 2005 by Thomas Nelson. Used by permission. All rights reserved.. | Scripture quotations marked NLT are taken from the *Holy Bible*, New Living Translation, copyright © 1996, 2004, 2015 by Tyndale House Foundation. Used by permission of Tyndale House Publishers, Inc., Carol Stream, Illinois 60188. All rights reserved. | Scripture taken from the New King James Version®. Copyright © 1982 by Thomas Nelson. Used by permission. All rights reserved.

First paperback edition February 2024

ISBN: 979-8-873-17125-5

theunstorableblessing.com

TABLE OF CONTENTS

Special Thanks v

Foreword vii

Introduction xi

1: It's Not What You Think 1

2: Changing Points of View 9

3: The Struggle is Real 15

4: Where The Struggle Comes From 27

5: The Treasure Effect 37

6: Aligning With A Limitless God 43

7: Living Under A Curse? 57

8: Living Under God's Limitless Blessing 65

9: The Difference Between Seeds and Bread 75

10: How To Receive The Unstorable Blessing 81

Conclusion 91

About the Author 93

SPECIAL THANKS TO:

My wife and family who have nudged me for years to start sharing through writing books.

Pastor Matt Keller who provided insight and practical help through the writing process.

Shay Jewett for hours *(and hours)* spent in research, proofreading and editing this content into the form of a book.

Dr. Jay Egbo for suggesting the title for the book after hearing one of my sermons that this book's content came from.

FOREWORD

It all started with $1.42.

I'll never forget the feeling. I was 15 years old and working at an ice cream shop just off the courthouse square of the little town I grew up in Indiana. I had said yes to a relationship with Jesus in the spring of that year and a few months later, I heard my Pastor preach a message on tithing for the first time.

That week, after working a few hours at the ice cream store, I received my paycheck for the grand total of $14.20 before taxes! When I got home, I remember going up to my childhood desk, opening the middle drawer and pulling out the checkbook I had gotten when my parents opened for me a "grown up bank account" earlier that year.

I remember writing in the amount: $1.42. One Dollar and 42/100.

The tithe.

10% of my increase.

I still remember the sound of the perforation as I tore it out. And then a day later I remember filling out the offering envelope for the very first time (complete with the taste of glue on my tongue from licking the little tab on the back!). When the purple offering bag came by, I took the envelope out of my Bible and put it inside. And in that moment, my life changed forever because of that first step of faith concerning my finances! (Though I never could have realized it then.)

Today, over 30 years later, my wife Sarah and I have been blessed to give away thousands of dollars for kingdom causes and to steward millions of dollars for His kingdom through the local church and ministries we lead. And the result has been, and continues to be, the impact we get to make on the eternities of people!

People are the ultimate reward. To think God lets us be a part of what He is doing on the earth today by stewarding finances for His glory is truly the greatest experience of our lives. And our heart is for every believer to experience that reality as well. That is why this book is so important. And David Wright is the right person to deliver this message.

It was a good day the first time I met David & Chereé Wright! You know how there are some people you meet and you just know, *"These people are special!"* Well, that's how I felt when I met them. Chereé lights up every room she is in and David, well, David is downright brilliant! In all my years of knowing David, there's never been a time where I have heard him teach that I have not left more in awe of God and with a greater depth and insight of what God's Word says and how it has the power to change my life!

That's how I feel about this book as well! David has a powerful gift to unpack and unlock the truth of Scripture and apply it to our lives in such a way that it doesn't just make logical sense - but is revelatory as well! That's what I believe is going to happen to you as you read this book. There are few things in life as near and dear to our heart as money and that's why God's Word has so much to say about how we manage and steward it. Each of us have been entrusted with a great responsibility; the management of the resources of heaven. They just happen to have American Presidents' faces on them. (And Alexander Hamilton as well, I know!)

What we do with what we have been given determines the course of our lives. That's why this book matters so much. I hope you'll not just read it, but actually slow down with the questions at the end of each chapter, have conversations about it with loved ones and friends and then most of all, act on what you've been entrusted to steward for the Lord. Then watch how God shows up in your life.

There is a way to experience the unstorable blessings of God in your life. This book tells you how!

Pastor Matt Keller
Founding and Lead Pastor of Next Level Church in Fort Myers, FL
Founder of the Next Level Relational Network of churches

INTRODUCTION

It was January of 2006 and we were in the perfect storm. My wife, Chereé, our 14-year-old daughter Lacie and I were facing the convergence of several major life developments – each of which would have been extremely difficult on their own.

Over the previous eight weeks, Chereé's Dad, Pastor Phil Howe went home to be with Jesus at 59 years of age, after a five-year fight with a neurological disorder called Lewy Body Disease. In addition to that, we had just completed a ministry assignment in the Phoenix area and were hoping to return to Dallas to resume working at the church we were previously serving. Employment transitions bring their own elements of uncertainty and all kinds of pressure with them. We needed direction, peace and provision from God. *And He is always faithful*.

A phone call to Dr. Lawrence Kennedy, the Pastor of the church in Dallas where we had served on staff, brought direction to us in the form of an impression from God during a time of prayer over us. In short, he said, "God's assignment for you to the congregation you were serving is complete. However, His purpose for you all in that region is not. Get a map of the Phoenix Valley out and ask God where He wants you to plant a church."

<u>We were shocked</u>! We never imagined - and definitely never desired to - plant a church. It was the last thing on our minds.

There we were, facing three truly difficult life developments: The passing of Chereé's father, a transition of employment, and an unanticipated ministry assignment. It seemed overwhelming. Yet we clearly heard God's direction and sensed His peace. Now it came down to God's provision. *And He is always faithful.*

The Pastor of the congregation we had served in an interim ministry role, very graciously and generously gave us a 90-day blessing check to help our family transition between assignments. While we were thanking God for this provision, Chereé said, "There it is." "There what is?" I replied. "The $5,000 we told God we would sow into the church building program if He brought it to us."

My mind flashed back to the previous April and the replay rolled. Sure enough, we'd made a pledge to God that if He provided a way for us to do so, we would sow $5,000 into that church's building program. It was clear to us that God had provided, so we wrote out a check in that amount and gave it back to that church's building fund just as we had pledged to do.

I admit, in the moment, *<u>it was a genuine struggle</u>* to let go of what amounted to such a large chunk of what was supposed to sustain our family for 90 days. But what I couldn't see at that point was what God was doing behind the scenes. *I had no idea <u>what following through on that offering</u> would enable Him to do through our lives from that moment forward.*

We didn't just barely squeak through the next 90 days on beans and rice. Quite the opposite in fact. In 90 really short days, God led us through a vision launch meeting with 30 adults and 20 kids in attendance. From that small vision launch party on Super Bowl Sunday of 2006, to our public launch service on Easter a few weeks later, God provided over $80,000 to purchase everything we needed to launch Life Link Church – *and from only people that were on the launch team.* <u>We never received $1 from outside funding</u>.

We were blown away with 254 people worshiping together on that Easter morning launch Sunday. On day one, people said yes to following Jesus (as have others almost every Sunday since). For the record, "eternal life-changing salvation" is the true treasure we cherish in this life. *However, the focus of this book is how God uses the "treasure effect" - and the struggle we work through in the process - to transform* **us** *"into His likeness" (see Romans 8:28-29).*

The financial effect of following through on that $5,000 offering has been staggering. In the few months that followed that offering, God provided everything we needed to launch Life Link Church. In addition to that, by the end of "90 days," the new church was strong enough financially to cover all the ongoing ministry operations which covered renting a worship facility and hiring staff - including us.

In fact, in that first year (2006), God's people brought over $400,000 into His kingdom through Life Link Church (the church we planted). Over the following years *we have had the incredible privilege of stewarding literally millions of dollars* to see thousands of people touched and prepared to see Jesus in eternity.

I shudder to think of what would have happened if Chereé and I had chosen to "hang onto that $5,000 offering" instead of sowing it. God provided it, we sowed it (admittedly through no small sense of struggle) and *He turned that $5,000 into millions of dollars that have flowed through our hands and influence* as Lead Pastors of Life Link Church.

We're not "special." We just followed the pathway outlined in this book. Doing so gave God (Who is constantly looking for people to work through like this) what He was looking for <u>in order to pour His "Unstorable Blessing" through</u> for His Kingdom purposes.

This pathway works equally well whether a person is working in a sacred calling like ministry or in a secular assignment. Throughout the book are stories of people that God has assigned to secular fields of employment who have experienced the same thing we have. In fact, the final story in chapter 10 is about the extraordinary experience of a businessman in the earthmoving industry. It doesn't get any more secular than manufacturing earthmoving equipment.

God uses our money struggles in a profound way. It's in our best interest to follow Him through the struggle. It is what aligns our hearts and lives with Him and His Kingdom in ways nothing else in this life will.

Let's talk about that struggle…

CHAPTER 1: IT'S NOT WHAT YOU THINK

Why is money such a struggle for so many people? Honestly, when we struggle with money, we often think it's actually the money we're struggling with. Frankly, currency is just a unique blend of fabric with exclusive ink and security features woven together into it. When we dig into the issue a little, we find that *money is not what the struggle is*. Rather, it <u>shows us what we're struggling with</u>. The struggle is real, it's just that dollars aren't the issue. Most of the time, it comes down to perspective, what we think or how we see things. Here's the way God describes reality from His (true) perspective:

> [8] *"For my thoughts are not your thoughts, neither are your ways my ways," declares the LORD.* [9] *"As the heavens are higher than the earth, so are my ways higher than your ways and my thoughts than your thoughts."*
>
> Isaiah 55:8-9 NIV

God isn't bragging. He's stating an actual truth. Why would God go out of His way to explain to us that His thoughts and ways are different and higher than our thoughts and ways? Probably for more reasons than we can ever know. But one of them would be this: He knows that we struggle in life against things we can't see and don't understand. However, He wants us to know that there is hope, there are answers, and there are truths we can live by that provide life-giving direction. And those truths are tied to Him.

He's basically saying, "Hey, I know there are times in life when you feel like you're tumbling around inside the drum of a clothes dryer. You can't tell which way is up or down." God wants us to know that just because we may feel disoriented, confused or out of sorts, that it doesn't mean we have to live that way. There actually is hope. There is truth, and we can know Him. He is truth.

There is a major difference between the way we see things and the way He sees things, the way we instinctively think about something and the way He thinks about it. And we get to select which perspective we base our choices on (which is exciting on one hand and terrifying on the other).

* *

When I was a kid, I grew up thinking, "I can't wait to be an adult because when I'm an adult, then I will get to do whatever I want to do." Well, I'm adulting now. And

I realize life is completely different as an adult than I ever imagined it would be when I was 12 years old.

I am harnessed with responsibilities, burdened with taxes, the list is long. And it is made up of all the things that a kid could never understand. Kids often look at adults and think, "I can't wait to be you," not knowing there are many times adults feel like, "Man, a peanut butter and jelly sandwich with no cares to stress about, and all I have to do is homework and watch TV when I'm done? Bring it on!"

* *

That's how childhood is. We misunderstand things that seem real to us but are not actually real at all. And we think that, "Someday we'll get what we want." Then, we grow up and get what we wanted, only to realize, "I don't actually want this."

So God says, "Let Me cut to the chase. I will tell you what is actually true and what truly works. You get to choose, *but, you get what you choose*." And by His grace, we stay alive long enough to realize what is actually true. At some point, it starts to sink in on us, "I guess my way isn't the best way. I should start listening to God and trusting His way."

Here is how Jesus describes the process He leads us through in order for us to discover truth - and the freedom that truth provides.

> [31] *To the Jews who had believed him, Jesus said, "If you hold to my teaching, you are*

really my disciples. ³² *<u>Then</u> you will know the truth, and the truth will set you free."*
John 8:31-32 NIV (author's emphasis)

In other words, God is saying, "In order to learn what is actually true, you have to functionally 'trust' truth first - and I am Truth." He is saying. "If you follow My teaching, <u>then</u> you will learn what is true. You will discover it. It will dawn on you. But don't wait for the truth to dawn on you before you trust and follow My instructions. You have to trust Me by following Me first. Along the way, it will dawn on you. You'll know the truth." And it's at the point you then "know the truth" *that the experience of freedom dawns in your soul and you realize, "I'm free from that."*

There is an element of dealing with money that we really do have to trust and follow God's directives first, while it doesn't "make sense," so that we can then learn/know the truth. When we discover that reality, it does several things for us. One of which is, it sets us free! The other thing it does for us is deepen our trust in Him. It dawns on us, "Since God is right about this, then He's probably right about the other things He tells us, too."

God wants us to know that how we deal with "treasure" in this life is more important and life-shaping than most of us think. In fact, it is part of something He is looking for as it relates to the way our lives align with His purposes. Notice the intention and motivation He reveals in this verse:

> ⁹ *For the eyes of the LORD (search) throughout the earth to strengthen (show himself faithful to) those whose hearts are fully committed to him.*
>
> *2 Chronicles 16:9a NIV*

We know that He came to seek and save those who were lost. But we get the understanding from this verse that, in all of what God is doing, He is also telling us, "Hey, I'm actively looking for something on the earth. I'm looking for those I can show Myself strong on behalf of."

Then God describes who that is. He says, "I'm looking for people who are fully committed to Me." He's not being an egocentric narcissistic. He's looking for people whose hearts are fully committed to Him - *so that **He can show Himself faithful to them**.*

So, we understand from the message of that verse that God is saying, "I want to show Myself faithful to people. I want to show Myself strong to people. I want to strengthen people." What He's implying is, "I want to do some things in those people that they cannot do themselves. I want to give them access to supernatural power. I want to give them access to unlimited (unstorable) resources. I want them to experience who I am in ways that blow their minds. But in order for Me to do that, they have to be fully committed to Me."

Why? Because if we are not fully submitted and committed to Him, our human nature will take everything He moves <u>to</u> us and consume it. We'll use it for ourselves.

God knows that we need things. He designed life to be experienced, for our bodies to be fueled, and our needs to be resourced. It's just that He wants to do far more than that in and through us.

God is telling us, "I'm looking. I'm searching. I want to find people whose hearts are fully committed to Me so that in that fully committed relationship, through that covenant, that selfless connection, I can pour extraordinary measures of Myself into them and it won't destroy them."

Who can He do that for? People who love and follow Him. Notice the response on our part that comes from loving Him.

> 15 *"If you love me, you will obey my commandments."*
>
> John 14:15 NCV

That message can be heard from two different perspectives. On the one hand, we can hear that as God saying, "Prove Your love to Me by doing what I say." That's actually how *we* tend to operate with each other. But that's not the way He operates.

On the other hand, He's actually saying, "If you love Me, if your life is anchored in a genuine relationship with Me, then you'll *know* Me and you will do what I'm saying because you *trust* Me." God is saying, "I'm looking for that alignment, that love, that trust, that obedience at a heart and motivational level, *so I can measure how much of Me and My power and resources I can pour back into you.*"

Many things in life actually work differently than they seem to at first. Take money for example. *People tend to love money*. But when you dig deeper into that idea a bit, you realize it isn't money they love so much. *What they love is what money represents*: the freedom to do what they want to do, when they want to do it, without answering to anyone else.

"It's my money. I'll do what I want to with it. If I want this, I'll get it. If I want that, I'll get that, too." Why? "I have the money to do whatever I want to do." *It's almost like money functions in God's role in their life*. But God says otherwise.

> [24] *"No one can serve two masters. Either you will hate the one and love the other, or you will be devoted to the one and despise the other. You cannot serve both God and money."*
>
> Matthew 6:24 NIV

We may try to fool ourselves about this, but God is telling us that it is actually impossible to love both God and money. We will love one or the other. We will be devoted to one or the other.

Again, the way we deal with "treasure" has a much bigger function in the way our lives work than most people realize. *But as we'll discover in the next chapter, in order to "see" this <u>treasure effect</u> more clearly, we'll need to change our point of view.*

REFLECTION QUESTIONS

1. *Consider the perspective presented in this chapter that money itself is not the actual struggle but rather reveals what individuals are struggling with. How does this perspective challenge common beliefs about financial challenges? Can you identify areas in your life where money has revealed deeper struggles or desires?*
2. *This chapter talks about the process of discovering truth and freedom through following Jesus' teachings. How have trusting and following God's directives led to a deeper understanding of truth and freedom in your life? Can you share a specific experience where following God's guidance resulted in newfound freedom?*
3. *This chapter highlights the idea that God is actively searching for those whose hearts are fully committed to Him - <u>for the purpose of showing Himself faithful to them</u>. How does this perspective challenge your understanding of God's role in your life?*
4. *The contrast between childhood perceptions and the realities of adulthood are discussed. Are there aspects of your life now that you once desired but realize you may not want now?*

CHAPTER 2: CHANGING POINTS OF VIEW

Perspective matters.

Here is an old illustration. As soon as you see it, you'll know exactly what the next point is going to be, but pretend you don't.

https://www.researchgate.net/profile/Jonathan-Schooler/publication/271842692/figure/fig3/AS:614224988479500@1523454057345/Rubins-vase-sometimes-referred-to-as-The-Two-Face-One-Vase-Illusion-depicts-the.png

If you focus on the black shape in the middle of that image, you can clearly see a vase. If you concentrate on the white elements on each side of the image, you clearly see two white faces in contrast. Now that you can "see both perspectives," you can actually switch back and forth between them in your mind's eye.

Using this illustration, let's apply that ability to "switch back and forth between two perspectives once you can see both of them" to the issue of <u>ownership</u> in life.

The basic question is, "Who actually owns what in this life?"

There's something about us that wants to own everything - because if we own it, **we can do whatever we want to with it**. Why? "It's mine."

"...whatever we WANT to..."

That's the root of the problem. We tend to make decisions based on our "wanter." The problem is our "wanter" is distorted.

If someone is asked the question, "How much is enough?", the most common answer is basically, "More." We might not know "how much more." We just instinctively want a little bit more."

Perhaps one of the most terrified people in history was King Solomon in the Old Testament of the Bible. He had absolutely everything a man could want. Everything: power, wealth, women, materials, kingdoms, he had it all. The Bible said he was the richest man ever. And, he could do anything he wanted to do - because he was the King. He had it all. And ultimately, he was the most miserable man ever because he realized at the end of his journey that "having it all" never truly fulfilled him.

Many times we think we're miserable *because we don't have enough money to get what we think we want*. So the illusion that keeps driving us forward through the maze of life is, "When I get that one, I'll be happy." "Oh, that didn't do it." "Then when I get that one, and when I get that raise, and then when I get that girl, or that guy, or that house, or that car, or that promotion, or that many social media followers, or this brand, or when I get that ..., then I'll be satisfied."

So we're driven and compelled through a maze of confusion by this force on the inside of us that is clamoring for just - more. It's called <u>materialism</u>. People who follow their "wanter" like that through life are truly miserable, in large part, because they think "I don't have 'it' yet." And God, in His benevolent mercy, is saying, "I don't want you to end up like Solomon. You'll never have it all, because 'having it all' leaves you, of all people, the most miserable - because you realize 'it' is never enough."

God wants us to know that the pursuit of stuff - for the benefit of owning it - is a lost cause before it starts. What is His solution? It begins by choosing to "live" from His perspective.

Notice the way He describes the difference between His point of view and ours.

> [8] *"For my thoughts are not your thoughts, neither are your ways my ways," declares the LORD.* [9] *"As the heavens are higher*

than the earth, so are my ways higher than your ways and my thoughts than your thoughts."

Isaiah 55:8-9 NIV

Now that God has helped us see that His thoughts and ways are different - and higher - than our thoughts and ways are (or our perspective), let's take a look at *why God allows us to struggle in this life and then one of the biggest things we struggle with:* "who" actually "owns" what.

REFLECTION QUESTIONS

1. *Reflect on the visual illustration of the vase and faces. How does this illustration resonate with the concept of perspective in your own life? Can you recall instances where changing your perspective led to a better understanding of a situation?*
2. *Isaiah 55:8-9 emphasizes the difference between God's thoughts and ways and human thoughts and ways. Reflect on moments in your life where you recognized the need to align your perspective with God's. How did this alignment impact your choices and outlook on life?*
3. *The chapter discusses the distorted nature of our "wanter." Consider your own desires and wants. How do you distinguish between genuine needs and distorted desires in your life?*
4. *King Solomon's story is highlighted as an example of someone who "had" everything but found himself ultimately unfulfilled. In what ways do you see parallels between Solomon's pursuit of fulfillment and common cultural attitudes toward success and materialism today?*

CHAPTER 3: THE STRUGGLE IS REAL

First of all, is struggle really supposed to be part of how life works? Short answer: yes. There is no escaping it. Struggle is a major part of life - but it also has constructive potential built into it. While we may initially want to avoid struggle, at some point we realize that strength, significance, fulfillment and most of life's more meaningful experiences are, in many ways, developed *through* the struggles we encounter along the way.

One of life's most important questions is, "What am I trusting for significance, security, and fulfillment in life?" For most people, *gathering and storing things we treasure* form the foundation of their answer to that question. It is interesting to realize that God doesn't downplay the importance of treasure. *But He does have a vitally important perspective about how treasure works in life*, especially the <u>way</u> we go about gathering and storing it.

Here is what Jesus said about that:

> [19] *"Do not store up for yourselves treasures on earth, where moths and vermin*

destroy, and where thieves break in and steal. ²⁰ *But store up for yourselves treasures in heaven, where moths and vermin do not destroy, and where thieves do not break in and steal."*
Matthew 6:19-20 NIV

God is saying, "Don't store treasures up for yourselves *here **on** earth*. *Instead*, (do) store treasures up *for yourselves **in** heaven*." (We'll cover how that works in another chapter.) Look carefully how Jesus describes the *effect* treasure has in our lives.

²¹ *"For where your treasure is, there your heart will be also."*
Matthew 6:21 NIV

The New International Version (NIV) highlights the emphasis Jesus placed on "*where* our hearts will be" (ie: where we store up treasures for ourselves.)

The New Living Translation (NLT) highlights the **"*element* within our heart"** that *ties it to our treasure*:

²¹ *"Wherever your treasure is, there the desires of your heart will also be."*
Matthew 6:21 NLT (author's emphasis)

And there it is: *Desire!* (one of life's biggest struggles).

Desire is mostly what motivates or "drives" people through life. God created us with the gift of desire. Can you imagine what life would be like without desire? Desire is a profound gift from God. It compels us in every dimension of who we are.

It's just that most people have never learned that desire can be *steered*. They actually just *follow* their desires.

You might be thinking, "Well, isn't that what you do with desire?" Yes, if you want to waste your life. But God created desire for something else: motivation to empower us to push through the struggles of life and grow into all He created for us to become.

What's important to recognize from Matthew 6:19-21 is that He also "identified how to actually 'steer' this seemingly uncontrollable thing called desire in our lives." God is helping us see that ***"the treasure effect" is what steers those desires***.

With that in mind, let's look at an aspect of life that seems to be one of the biggest struggles of all: "who" owns "what"? *(Buckle your seatbelts, the ride may get bumpy...)*

Psalm 24:1 NIV starts off like this:

> [1] *The earth is the LORD'S, and everything in it...*

Many people may think, "Okay, I can buy that so far. God can have the earth. I don't want it. I don't want Saturn, or anything else in the cosmos either."

It's the next phrase that tends to bother just about everyone at first:

> [1] *The earth is the LORD'S, and everything in it, <u>the world, and all who live in it</u>.*
> *Psalm 24:1 NIV (author's emphasis)*

Let that sink in for a minute. He's not just talking about cows, and horses, and eagles, and whales. All who live in it includes <u>*all, which means, ultimately, us*</u>. To which most people respond, "Nobody owns me. I own me."

God is telling us, "Hey, pay attention. I own it all - including you. You and everything under your influence is Mine." **That's where the struggle comes from.**

We may think, "Well, that's the Old Testament. We live in the New Testament era." Well let's just open that New Testament to 1 Corinthians 6:19 and see what God tells us in that passage.

> [19] *Do you not know that your bodies are temples of the Holy Spirit, who is in you, whom you have received from God? <u>You are not your own</u>;* [20] *you were bought at a price...*
> *1 Corinthians 6:19-20a NIV*
> *(author's emphasis)*

In Psalm 24 and other passages of scripture, God declares, "I'm the creator. I own everything. I own everything in the cosmos, the universe. I own it all. I created it. It's all Mine."

But look at the perspective God shows us in the passage in 1 Corinthians. "<u>**You**</u> were bought at a price." Now God is talking about something besides your body. Now He's articulating the fact that <u>*you*</u>, not just the body you live in, are His.

We start life unredeemed, on our own, separated from God, driving the earth suit we live in through reality as we know it - the best we can, until we figure out that *we really do need to experience the life-transforming grace* of our Savior and then surrender "our" lives to Jesus. In that miraculous moment, our spirit is reconnected with God in a way that takes us from death to life, and then we "live" linked in relationship with Him. God describes that process as being born again.

Now, let's look at how God completes the thought He shares with us in 1 Corinthians 6:19-20 NIV.

> [19] *Do you not know that your bodies are temples of the Holy Spirit, who is in you, whom you have received from God? You are not your own;* [20] *you were bought at a price. Therefore honor God with your bodies.*
>
> *1 Corinthians 6:19-20 NIV*

People may think, "<u>**Your**</u> bodies? I thought everything belonged to God." <u>Here is an important nuance people sometimes miss</u>.

Let's say someone asks you to assist them by taking a $100.00 bill from their hand to a person sitting on the other side of the room. How hard would that be to do? Not hard at all. Why? *That $100.00 bill was never "yours" to begin with.* It was, however, in "your hands" for a few moments.

Here's where "your" touches the things around you. It's "your choice" in how you handle what God has put into "your influence."

That's the one thing God won't do for us. Everything else, He does. It's the "our choice" that makes it "ours." So the body we live in is **not ours** to feed it what we *want* it fed, to sex it the way we *want* it sexed, to entertain it the way we *want* it entertained, etc.

God is saying, especially for the redeemed, but in every other way, too, *"That's not yours, but you are treating it as if it's yours. So,* **the reason you are struggling is because you think it's yours.**"

Our struggle isn't because of what is true. *The struggle is because of how we think about what is in "our hands."* If we think it's <u>ours</u>, we tend to do whatever <u>we want to do</u> with it. God is saying, "It isn't yours except for one thing: what you choose to do with it (how you manage it). That's the 'yours' part of it."

In 1 Corinthians 6:19-20, God is saying, "The body I put under your management, I want you to use for My glory."

The best way to respond to that scripture is to say, "God, this body is Yours. I will do with it what You want done with it, for Your glory, for Your purpose." Why? "Because it's not mine."

Someday, we'll shed the earth suits we live in. Then the actual "us" will step into eternity shaped the way we <u>chose</u> to be shaped (by the way we responded to God's direction throughout our lives).

Jesus amplified it a bit more as He was teaching about this in the New Testament.

> [15] *Then he said, "Beware! Guard against every kind of greed. Life is not measured by how much you own."* [16] *Then he told them a story: "A rich man had a fertile farm that produced fine crops.* [17] *He said to himself, 'What should I do? I don't have room for all my crops.'"*
>
> *Luke 12:15-17 NLT*

The man made a factually true statement. "I don't have room for all 'my' crops." Remember, Jesus is using this parable to warn against the deceptive power of greed. Note: Greed only has power over what a person **believes** is "theirs" or something "they **have a right to have or experience**..." In this parable, the man arrived at a solution that would be a "natural" one for many people who believe the things in "their possession" are "theirs."

> [18] *Then he said, "I know! I'll tear down my barns and build bigger ones. Then I'll have room enough to store all my wheat and other goods."*
>
> *Luke 12:18 NLT*

Did you catch that? "My wheat…" Verse 19 gives us the context of which "perspective" of "my wheat" he was operating from.

> [19] *"And I'll sit back and say to myself, 'My friend, you have enough stored away for years to come. Now take it easy! Eat, drink, and be merry!'"*
> Luke 12:19 NLT

This man was clearly not operating from the perspective that the wheat in "his hands" *actually belonged to God who had entrusted it into his hands to manage for God's purposes and on His behalf.*

Next, Jesus tells the man that he'd been fooled (deceived). As a result, <u>he had missed the whole point of life</u>.

> [20] *"But God said to him, 'You fool! You will die this very night. Then who will get everything you worked for?'"*
> Luke 12:20 NLT

Jesus was using that illustration to teach the point, "Don't throw your life away pursuing material gains as if that's going to do something for you. The only thing that approach will do is absorb your life and suck time out of your equation until there's nothing left for you to actually choose with. And then you will step into eternity realizing, 'I've chosen wrongly.'"

Don't pursue stuff for the sake of owning it so you can do whatever you want to with it. It isn't yours to begin with, and that very mindset itself is the problem.

Then Jesus wrapped up the parable by refocusing on the truth from His perspective.

> [21] *"Yes, a person is a fool to store up earthly wealth but not have a rich relationship with God."*
>
> *Luke 12:21 NLT*

Here's what Jesus was **not** saying. He was not saying that, "A person is a fool to handle a lot of money." The point of the parable is that, "A person is a fool if they spend their life *pursuing* money, not God."

Here's the truth. When we pursue God first, we get Him and everything else anyway.

Is it possible the reason God doesn't just dump resources on most of us is that He knows we would consume ourselves into oblivion with them? It's as if <u>He measures out just enough resources to match our character maturity</u>.

* *

Note: If, as you are reading along, it is clear to you that you do not have a "rich relationship" with God, I want you to know, you were made for that. And deep down inside, you know it. I believe that, in your heart, you actually want to start that relationship with God but may not know how to start that with Him. If that is the case, here are words to pray that your heart is already saying to God. Pray them aloud with all your heart:

Heavenly Father, I acknowledge that You are God and I am not. I want to thank You for loving me enough to tell me the truth in Your Bible.

Lord Jesus, thank You for loving me enough to die on Calvary's cross, giving Your sinless life as a ransom for me. I confess I need Your salvation and ask that You forgive me for every sin in my life. I ask You to wash me, cleanse me and make me new. Right now, I surrender my whole life to You. I choose to follow You as my only Lord and Savior for the rest of my life.

Holy Spirit, come into my heart and give me the strength I'll need to live for Jesus all my life.

In Jesus' Name I pray, amen.

Congratulations on making the most important decision of your life. Welcome to the Family of God!

It is really important to connect with a Bible-based, Christ-centered local church in your area and walk out the rest of God's great plan for you in relationship with other Christ-followers who can help you along the way.

My wife (Chereé) and I lead Life Link Church in Gilbert, AZ (SE Phoenix Valley - lifelinkchurch.com). We would be thrilled to be part of your new journey with Jesus if you are close enough to our area and don't already relate to a Bible-based, Christ-centered church. If you do relate with a church like that, reach out to them and tell them about your decision to follow Jesus. They'll come alongside of you and get you off and running in your new life in Christ.

If you don't already relate with a church like that, you can connect with us by texting CONNECT to 480-470-0800 and follow the prompts from there. Let us know you just committed your life to following Jesus while reading this book. We'll reach out and connect with you for a great new start.

If you are not in our area and don't happen to know of a church like that near you, we have friends that lead great churches in lots of places. We would be honored to help you get connected with them. Just connect with us by texting CONNECT to 480-470-0800 and follow the prompts from there to let us know. We'll get right on it!

* *

Now that we've settled the biggest "ownership" issue in this life, let's take a closer look at where the struggle actually comes from.

REFLECTION QUESTIONS

1. *How does the concept of struggle being an inherent part of life resonate with your personal experiences? Can you recall specific instances where struggles contributed to personal growth or development?*
2. *This chapter discusses desire as a significant aspect of human life and suggests that many people simply follow their desires instead of steering them. Can you give an example of when you "followed" a desire into an undesirable outcome in stead of "steering" that desire in a more constructive way?*
3. *Psalm 24:1 asserts that "the earth is the Lord's, and everything in it." How does the idea that everything, including ourselves, belongs to God challenge your perception of ownership and control in your life? How might this perspective influence your decision-making?*
4. *The chapter concludes with the importance of pursuing a rich relationship with God over earthly wealth. Reflect on your priorities and aspirations. How central is your relationship with God in comparison to other pursuits in your life?*

CHAPTER 4: WHERE THE STRUGGLE COMES FROM

Yes, the struggle is definitely real - bafflingly so. But it doesn't have to stay cloaked in mystery. God tells us in James 4:1-3 exactly what causes so much of our struggles.

> *¹ What causes fights and quarrels among you? Don't they come from your desires that battle within you? ² You desire but do not have, so you kill. You covet but you cannot get what you want, so you quarrel and fight...*
>
> *James 4:1-2a NIV*

God went out of His way to let people know what causes fights and quarrels. He points out that it is our **desires** that battle within us. Self-centered, self-serving desires cause fights and quarrels - the majority of our struggle. Then He makes this statement:

> ² *... You do not have because you do not ask God.*
>
> *James 4:2b NIV*

There is a good chance that you have heard that statement before, but slow down and thoughtfully read that sentence again. "You do not have because you do not ask God."

You may have just thought, "Not true! I ask Him for stuff all the time and don't receive it."

Okay. But there are two applications that are being identified in this passage (one more obvious than the other).

The first application is outlined in verse three.

> ³ *When you ask, you do not receive, because you ask with wrong motives, that you may spend what you get on your pleasures (desires).*
>
> *James 4:3 NIV*

So He's basically saying, "If you are asking for something in order to satisfy a desire that you think will fulfill you, but I know that it won't, I am not going to give you that."

"Fair enough," you might say. "What is the other application God is pointing out in this passage?"

Again, look carefully at the second half of James 4 verse 2 (NIV),

> ² *... You do not have because you do not ask God.*

Here's a perspective that may not be as obvious. Another application of what God is stating here could be said like this: *"Part of why you don't 'have' (what you believe you need) is because <u>you have spent what I put in your hands before you asked Me about it</u>. So when it's time for you to 'get what you need,' you have already spent what I put in your hands knowing the need was coming."*

So He's not saying, "You don't have the stuff that you want because you're not asking for it." He says, "You're actually not letting Me guide your spending. You're letting your desires direct your spending."

In other words, if you "want" a new purse, you "get" a new purse. If you "want" new shorts, you "get" new shorts. If you "want" new shoes, you "get" new shoes. If you "want" a new car, you "get" a new car - because you "want" to - *<u>and the resources to buy them are within your hands</u>*.

If we spend what we have '"now" on what we want, without asking God for His guidance on how to spend what is already in our hands, *it is highly likely that we will spend those resources on something we "want now" so they (the resources) are already out of our reach when "something we need" shows up*.

God is saying, "You have not because you don't ask Me. If you'd have asked Me, I'd have said, 'Don't buy those shoes.' Why? 'Because I know something that is coming you're going to actually need that money for. I'm putting a resource in your hand before you see the need or opportunity, so that when it shows up the resources you need for it are still in your hand.'"

Is God against getting new stuff? No, He's not against getting new stuff.

What He is looking for is the **opportunity** to get the immense, stored up wealth of the wicked actually *transferred* into our hands for *His borderless purposes* - without it destroying us!

God is showing us something profound through this section of scripture in James 4:1-3.

Our _unsubmitted desires_ are what _limits_ the resources God can put into our hands.

If we choose our way through life based on _what we want_, then God knows He can't actually provide what He wants to move through us because we'll mistake that as His provision for something that we want (and that He knows won't fulfill us). It'll just be more stuff.

God actually *is* looking for people that He can move unimaginable resources through.

* *

I once had someone tell me that they asked God every day to help them win the lottery so they could tithe and give a lot of money to the church. They lived a long life and ultimately passed away having never won the lottery, wondering, "If God owns it all, and is able to do anything, why wouldn't He do that for me?" Only God truly knows that answer. But history shows that the majority of people who come into reality-shifting wealth all of the sudden end up bankrupt within just a few years. Why? _**Because money is not the actual issue**_.

I believe in our generation, we will actually see with our eyes people just like us handle millions of dollars for the sake of God's purposes in the earth. I don't mean they have a million as net worth. I'm talking about millions coming in and they take those millions and say, "Here, for Your Kingdom, God, I'm putting these millions into where You lead me to put them."

* *

There will be people who get to the place with God that He says, "Now you're ready. *Your 'wanter' is truly under submission and unprecedented resources won't destroy you through consumption.* So, here's $3 million to handle for Me. Return My (holy) tithe to Me through your local church. Then I want you to give $1 million to your local church for My purpose there. Next I want you to send $1 million to 'that' ministry or charity for My purpose. Then I want you to send $1/2 million to 'that' ministry or charity for My purpose and I want you to budget the remaining $200,000 for your personal household needs over the next year."

At that point, we would say, "Awesome, God! Okay. Here's Your $300,000 tithe back to You through my local church. And here's the $1 million you led me to give to my local church for Your purposes. Here's another $1 million to 'that' ministry or charity for Your purposes. And another $1/2 million to 'that' ministry or charity for Your purposes. Now, I will budget the remaining $200,000 for my personal household over the next year."

You may have just heard the thought, "You mean all I'd 'get' out of $3,000,000 is a measly $200,000?"

(See what I'm talking about?)

What limits God's limitless provisions? *Our unsubmitted desires* (a heart that is not fully submitted to Him).

Gain ≠ Gain

Listen to the insight God gives us in this scripture:

> ⁶ *But godliness with contentment is great gain.* ⁷ *For we brought nothing into the world, and we can take nothing out of it.* ⁸ *But if we have food and clothing, we will be content with that.* ⁹ *Those who* <u>want to get rich</u> *fall into temptation and a trap and into many foolish and harmful desires that plunge people into ruin and destruction.* ¹⁰ *For the love of money is a root of all kinds of evil. Some people, eager for money, have wandered from the faith and pierced themselves with many griefs.*
> *1 Timothy 6:6-10 NIV (author's emphasis)*

In God's Kingdom, "great gain" (gaining more "stuff") does NOT equal the *experience of great gain*. He is very clear: GODLINESS (Values/Actions that reflect God and His way of life) **with** CONTENTMENT = GREAT GAIN.

This is not "easy" to achieve, but it actually is "simple" to understand.

Instinctively, it seems that "great gain should be great gain." And God repeats, "No, <u>**godliness**</u> (God-likeness) <u>**with contentment**</u> **is** great gain." Why? Because a God-like mindset or perspective is a generous perspective. That means when we have submitted our heart/desires to God, *He is able to remove the protective limits on His provision in our lives*. We are then able to do anything that He needs done. At that point, we are not limited by anything and are content to let God actually meet our true needs without turning His provisions into a self-serving "want" list.

God is basically saying, "<u>*This life is not about this life*</u>. Don't spend your life trying to store up treasure and experiences you think will satisfy you in this lifetime. You came into it naked, with nothing. You are leaving naked, with nothing. You can't take anything in this world with you."

Two things about this reality.

The first is this. What stewarding or handling resources on God's behalf does for us is give us the ability to *learn how to follow what He wants done and facilitate it - <u>in spite of our desires</u>*. So the whole thing of life is learning how to say this to our desires, "Not my will, but God's be done."

Secondly, we can take nothing out of this life <u>*except the character formation*</u> that happens as we choose to submit to (and actually live for) God and His Kingdom.

God is telling us, "Look, you're going to steward lots of resources during your lifetime on earth. Don't think you own those resources - as if they are yours to hold onto or hoard for your own sense of significance or security." Why? "Because they are just resources, and I use resources to accomplish My will on the earth. You came with nothing, you're going to leave with nothing. But when you steward My resources *My way* during this life, it shapes you to become more and more like Me (Romans 8:28-29)."

REFLECTION QUESTIONS

1. *Consider the statement, "You do not have because you do not ask God" (James 4:2b). How does this challenge common perceptions about acquiring what we need or desire? Describe an instance where seeking God's guidance before making a decision could have made a difference in your life.*
2. *Explore the idea that spending resources based on personal desires without seeking God's guidance can lead to missed opportunities or inadequate provision when needs arise. Reflect on your spending habits and consider how intentional consultation with God might impact your financial decisions.*
3. *Consider the concept that **unsubmitted desires are limits on God's provision**. In what areas of your life are your desires not fully submitted to God? How might surrendering these desires lead to a greater flow of God's resources and blessings in your life?*
4. *Reflect on the vision of individuals handling millions of dollars for God's purposes, as mentioned in this chapter. How does this challenge conventional views on wealth and prosperity? What steps can you take to align your heart with God's purpose for financial resources?*

5. *Consider the equation presented in 1 Timothy 6:6-10, emphasizing that godliness with contentment allows for the removal of limits on God's provision. In what ways can you cultivate godliness and contentment in your life? How might these qualities lead to a more generous and open-handed approach to resources?*

CHAPTER 5: THE TREASURE EFFECT

God works in ways that are truly baffling. Remember the way God describes the difference between _His_ perspective and methods and _our_ perspective and methods:

> [8] *"For my thoughts are not your thoughts, neither are your ways my ways," declares the LORD.* [9] *"As the heavens are higher than the earth, so are my ways higher than your ways and my thoughts than your thoughts."*
>
> *Isaiah 55:8-9 NIV*

As that applies to the way we handle treasure and resources during our lives, <u>more than one thing is happening at a time</u>. In a way that only God can operate, look at what He shows us through 1 Timothy 6:7 and Matthew 6:19-20.

> [7] *For we brought nothing into the world, and we can take nothing out of it.*
>
> *1 Timothy 6:7 NIV*

> [19] *"Do not store up for yourselves treasures on earth, where moths and vermin destroy, and where thieves break in and steal.* [20] *But (instead) store up for yourselves treasures in heaven, where moths and vermin do not destroy, and where thieves do not break in and steal."*
> Matthew 6:19-20 NIV

Notice: We can "take nothing out of the world." But we _can "store up for ourselves" treasures in heaven_.

In fact, if you look closely at Matthew 6:20, Jesus is *actually directing* us to do just that.

An obvious question, then, is, "How do I get treasure from here on earth to be 'stored up in heaven'?" Especially when we consider that our natural tendency is to hang onto treasure and keep it close to us in life. The first step in that process is to notice what Jesus illustrated in a parable found in the New Testament book of Luke. We have already learned our way through this parable in chapter 2, but let's take a closer look as we learn through it again.

> [15] *Then he said to them, "Watch out! Be on your guard against all kinds of greed; life does not consist in an abundance of possessions."* [16] *And he told them this parable: "The ground of a certain rich man yielded an abundant harvest.* [17] *He thought to himself, 'What shall I do? I have no place to store my crops.'* [18] *"Then he said, 'This is*

The Unstorable Blessing

what I'll do. I will tear down my barns and build bigger ones, and there I will store my surplus grain. [19] *And I'll say to myself, "You have plenty of grain laid up for many years. Take life easy; eat, drink and be merry."* [20] *"But God said to him, 'You fool! This very night your life will be demanded from you. Then who will get what you have prepared for yourself?'* [21] *"This is how it will be with whoever stores up things for themselves but is not rich toward God."*

Luke 12:15-21 NIV

Again, here's a summary of what Jesus illustrated. The man in this parable had a harvest (increase) that was too big for his storage system. His instinctive solution was to build bigger storage for all his harvest (increase). He never considered that God provided "more" as his harvest (increase) for <u>the benefit of others</u>. Instead, because his heart was self-centered, <u>he decided that he would increase his storage so he would be "set for life."</u> It must have been a complete shock, then, when Jesus told him bluntly, "You missed the whole point of life."

Jesus wanted them to understand that creating bigger capacity to store up treasure here in this life is a waste of this life. In other words, Jesus is saying, "What I want you to **be** is <u>*a pipeline*</u> for the resources I bring into your hands to manage. *That way, everything that moves 'through' you as I direct it for My purposes on the earth* *is 'accomplishing those purposes' AND actually 'being stored up **for you** in heaven' at the same time."*

Remember what God warned us about in 1 Timothy chapter 6.

> [9] *Those who <u>want</u> to get rich fall into temptation and a trap and into many foolish and harmful desires that plunge people into ruin and destruction.* [10] *For the love of money is a root of all kinds of evil. Some people, eager for money, have wandered from the faith and pierced themselves with many griefs.*
> 1 Timothy 6:9-10 NIV (author's emphasis)

Do you recognize how God is describing the "wanter" in that passage?

The direction and intent of our wanter is what limits God's ability to pour more and more blessing through us.

Notice: Money in itself is not evil. The <u>love of</u> money is a root of all kinds of evil.

Look at the potential outcome of those who live with that mindset: "Some people eager for (or wanting more) money have wandered from the faith and pierced themselves with many griefs." In other words, they want more money so badly that they ignore God's directives and actually chase after money (as if it can give them what they truly need). And in doing so they have pierced themselves with many griefs.

What do those griefs look like? Here's one way God describes those griefs:

> [5] *This is what the LORD of Heaven's Armies says: "Look at what's happening to you!* [6] *You have <u>planted</u> much <u>but harvest little</u>. You <u>eat</u> <u>but are not satisfied</u>. You <u>drink but are still thirsty</u>. You <u>put on clothes</u> but <u>cannot keep warm</u>. Your <u>wages disappear as though you were putting them in pockets filled with holes</u>!"*
> Haggai 1:5-6 NLT (author's emphasis)

Which is why God couldn't pour unlimited resources into them; it would destroy them.

In hindsight, it is in our best interest that the Lord does not respond to our misaligned requests (or even demands) for money. He knows exactly what the limit of His "unlimited" resources is that we can handle at every stage of our lives.

This leads us to ask, "How can I increase the limits of what God can constructively pour into my life?" In the next chapter, we will look at how we can align our lives to God in exactly that way.

REFLECTION QUESTIONS

1. *Reflect on Isaiah 55:8-9 and the profound difference between God's thoughts and ways and our human thoughts and ways. How does this understanding influence your approach to managing treasure and resources in your life?*
2. *Consider the parable in Luke 12:15-21 about the rich man with an abundant harvest. Reflect on your own attitudes toward wealth and possessions. Are you more inclined to build bigger storage for yourself, or do you see the resources in your hands as a means to benefit others and serve God's purposes?*
3. *Contemplate the idea that God wants us to be a thoroughfare for the resources He brings into our hands, allowing them to flow through us for His purposes. How does this perspective reshape your understanding of stewardship, generosity, and the purpose of accumulating resources?*
4. *Consider the outcome described in Haggai 1:5-6 for those who are consumed by the love of money. How does this serve as a cautionary tale about the potential consequences of misaligned priorities? In what ways can you ensure that your pursuit of financial success does not lead to dissatisfaction and unfulfillment?*

CHAPTER 6: ALIGNING WITH A LIMITLESS GOD

We first looked at this reality back in chapter 3.

> ¹ *The earth is the LORD's, and everything in it, the world, and all who live in it.*
> *Psalm 24:1 NIV*

In this chapter, we'll look into something that may seem a bit strange the first time you read it, so read the next sentence at least a couple times.
There is a "unique something" that is <u>part</u> of everything that belongs to God.
He calls it His tithe, and wants you to know it is a part of "everything" that is already His.

> ³⁰ *A tithe of everything from the land, whether grain from the soil or fruit from the trees, belongs to the LORD...*
> *Leviticus 27:30a NIV*

God is specifically pointing something out. He's saying, "I know that it's all Mine, but I want you to know there's a part of what is 'all Mine' that is '<u>**Mine in a different way**</u>.' I call it the tithe."

Listen to His next phrase.

> [30] *A tithe of everything from the land, whether grain from the soil or fruit from the trees, belongs to the LORD; <u>it is holy to the LORD</u>.*
> *Leviticus 27:30 NIV (author's emphasis)*

God is saying, "There's a dimension of reality attached to the holy part I call My tithe that's not attached to everything else that is also Mine. I want you to know what it is. That part is **holy to Me**."

Notice what He tells us to do with His tithe:

> [19] *The first of the firstfruits (the tithe) of your land you shall <u>bring</u> into the house of the LORD your God.*
> *Exodus 23:19a NKJV (author's emphasis)*

Did you notice He says "bring" and not "give?" Why? <u>**Because we can't "give" what isn't ours to begin with**</u>.

God wants us to know, "I own it all. But I have attached something to *that part* - the tithe - that is different. There is something attached to that part that nothing else touches. That part has a unique function between us. That part is holy, and I want you to bring that part to the House of the Lord, Your God."

So the first fruits, the tithe, must be returned. We don't "give" the tithe. We "bring" it. We "return" it.

Notice how God specifies what we are to do with the different elements He places in our hands.

First, He says to:

> ⁹ *Honor the LORD with your possessions...*
> *Proverbs 3:9a NKJV*

God has already established that He "owns" everything which means we don't own it. So when God uses the phrase, "your possessions," He is referring to things He has "placed into our hands - our control or management." God says, "Honor Me with all of that."

The question, then, is, "How do we *honor the Lord with **our** possessions*?"

* *

I saw a perfect example of this at a meeting I was in recently. Our men's leadership team was debriefing after one of our annual retreats. It was a fun meeting because the retreat was absolutely fantastic. It just happened to be right before Thanksgiving that year - which meant we didn't even have time to reset our personal lives before we were all plunging headfirst into the year-end holiday season. Everyone was still pretty spent from putting the retreat on.

One thing we needed to do in that meeting was to plan the following year's events. We all thought that starting the year with a Bacon Championship contest would be fun. The Men's Ministry Leader asked, "Who would be willing to host the event at their place?"

Crickets...

Everyone was suddenly absorbed in the arduous task of taking extremely detailed notes. It was awkwardly silent for way too long. Unfazed, the leader simply repeated, "Who would be willing to host the event at their place?"

More notes...

Again, "Who would be willing to host the event at their place?"

I couldn't take it any longer and said out loud in a bit-too-strong of a leadership voice, "Roger, he's talking about you and your house!"

Laughter - and relief - swept the room. Amazingly, everyone completed their annotation at that same moment, simply thrilled that Roger had "volunteered his house."

Roger was all smiles and said, "Absolutely!" (almost like it was all his own idea). The meeting got right back in motion like nothing had ever happened. While the guys were brainstorming the best Bacon Championship ever, I leaned over to Roger sitting beside me and said, "Hey Roger. I didn't even consider your personal life and the rhythm of your household when I said that. I can redirect that and fix it for you right now..."

He didn't even let me finish trying to let him off the hook. Without skipping a beat, he said, "*Pastor, that is God's house. He can use it any time and for anything He needs it for!"* I heard the sound of God's Kingdom resonating in his voice.

He told me later, *"When people compliment the nice big home we live in now, I make it a point to tell them, 'It's all from God. When we first started out in married life together, money was so tight we lived in a tiny, one-bedroom apartment. We had two plates, two forks and two spoons. We had no furniture and our bed was a blanket on the floor.'"*

There is an obvious reason the blessings of the Lord flow so clearly in Roger's family.

* *

Again, God specifies what we are to do with the different elements He places in our hands.

First, He says to:

> [9] *Honor the LORD with your possessions...*
> Proverbs 3:9a NKJV

Next, He clarifies the second type of element by what He points out in the rest of that verse.

> [9] *Honor the LORD with your possessions,*
> <u>*and with the firstfruits of all your increase*</u>.
> Proverbs 3:9 NKJV (author's emphasis)

Notice what is not included with "your possessions" <u>by virtue of being specifically called out in the last half</u>

of that sentence, *"And with the first fruits of all Your increase."* God is saying, "Honor Me with everything that you have in your control. Remember, just because it's in your hands doesn't mean you own it. It all belongs to Me and I want you to honor Me with that. I also want you to honor Me with the first fruits (My tithe)."

So, in His way of explaining it: everything is all His. *But there is* <u>*both*</u> *an "all your possessions" and a "first fruits" we have in our hands.* **Two different types of elements**.

We honor God with "our possessions" and "the first fruits (His tithe)" by doing what He says to do with them.

Once more, what does He say to do with His tithe (the first fruits)? Return it - bring it to the house of the Lord (your local church).

Why is God so focused on how we handle that first fruit of our increase? Among other things:

1. It is holy to Him.
2. The first portion, the tithe, is the redemptive portion.
3. The desires of our heart "follow" where we choose to direct our treasure.

[21] "Wherever your *treasure is*, <u>*there*</u> *the desires of your heart will also be."*
  Matthew 6:21 NIV (author's emphasis)

In the Old Testament of God's Bible, He gave His people these instructions. The firstborn of each of your livestock was to be sacrificed if it was designated as a "clean" animal. If the animal was designated as an "unclean" animal, it had to be redeemed by the sacrifice of a clean, spotless lamb. Those are the only two options God gave them - sacrifice or redemption. In either case, the owner was surrendering the first one (or its redemptive substitute) back to God.

In the New Testament, God provides a gripping illustration of that same principle through the life of Jesus. One day, John the Baptist was baptizing people in the Jordan River. When he recognized Jesus had walked up to be baptized, John declared, "Behold! The Lamb of God who takes away the sin of the world!" (John 1:29). John, in his inspired declaration, perfectly captured the role Jesus had come to earth to fulfill. Jesus, God's *firstborn* Son, was "clean" (sinless and unblemished in every way.)

In a way that parallels how we see God working in the Old Testament, Jesus - the spotless Lamb - had to be sacrificed in order to redeem all of us who were all born "unclean" with a fully-functioning sin nature. When Jesus gave His life as the redemptive payment for our sin, He purchased us back (redeemed us) for God. In a profound way, Jesus was God the Father's tithe.

God was demonstrating a powerful principle for us. It's like He said, "Hey, everybody. This is how life in My kingdom actually works. I gave you My very first (and only) to redeem you back from sin and death." That's what real love looks like.

> [8] *But God showed his great love for us by sending Christ to die for us while we were still sinners.*
> Romans 5:8 NIV

It is like God is saying, "I gave My first (and only and best) for you. I'm telling you that so you'll understand that the first part, the tithe, is holy to Me (it has a unique function). And it's not because I'm grumpy. I'm trying to show you something that's important to understand about how My kingdom works."

God doesn't actually need our money. (He paves heaven's streets with gold...) It is the "treasure element" of money that He responds to. He provides us with money (which we naturally treasure - but are not compelled to love). He then went out of His way to show us that the "treasure element" of money has a profound function in the deepest part of who we are as people - *our desires.*

> [21] *"<u>Wherever</u> your treasure is, <u>there</u> the desires of your heart will also be."*
> Matthew 6:21 NIV (author's emphasis)

Notice that the "treasure element" of money actually provides us with a way to "steer" <u>what is otherwise uncontrollable</u>: the "desires" of our heart.

Why is that so important? Because Proverbs 4:23 specifically says that the experience of our life is determined by the function of our heart.

> [23] *Guard your heart above all else, for it determines the course of your life.*
>
> Proverbs 4:23 NIV

God is telling us, "I gave you a way to steer your heart because I want you to know your heart affects everything you experience in life."

Since God's tithe is holy to Him and has a unique function in the way we relate with Him, how do we identify <u>which part</u> of what comes into our hands (the increase) <u>*is His tithe*</u>?

Let's say that you had a garage sale, or a birthday that ended up with you having $100 in ten-dollar bills that you didn't have before. You've had an "increase" of $100. God sees that and recognizes that one of those ten-dollar bills is already His - and He calls it the "first of the firstfruits" (His holy tithe). Since that is the one He calls holy, which ten-dollar bill is it?

Many times, we tend to think, "Well, let me get all my bills paid, all my weekend recreation done, watch all the movies I want to watch, and my subscriptions I want to pay for, and the extra clothes I need to buy and the restaurants I want to go to, and then at the end of that, I'll give God either what's left (if there is anything left) or the 10% that I just saved at the end of me doing whatever I want…"

But how can we actually know <u>which</u> 10% is actually His holy tithe? ***The first one out of your hand is the "first" of the firstfruits*** (as He describes it in His Bible).

As such, many people _live_ in God's tithe... Many people _are driving_ God's tithe. Many people _eat_ God's tithe. You get the picture...

You're like, "Surely He doesn't care."

What God wants us to know and understand is that He is real and His Kingdom ways really work - all the time.

Our ignorance of how they work (or rejection or rebellion to the way they work) doesn't keep His Kingdom laws from working in our lives. They operate consistently the way He designed them to work regardless of what we think or choose to do.

It's like God is saying, "Please get this. I really want to do more in you, for you, and through you than you could ever imagine. But I'm the only one that can see the condition of your heart as it actually is. You don't know what's in there. So when I tap on something and a weed that you can recognize pops up, you then have the opportunity to decide how to respond to what I illuminated for you."

Notice what God points out in verse 10 of Proverbs chapter 3.

> [9] *Honor the LORD with your wealth, with the firstfruits of all your crops;* [10] ***then your barns will be filled to overflowing****, and* *your vats will brim over with new wine*.
> Proverbs 3:9-10 NIV (author's emphasis)

What's He saying? When we honor the Lord with our possessions <u>and</u> with the first fruits of all of our increase, He has 100% of our hearts. So, He can pour more resources into, for, and through us than we need, because we've already demonstrated that we live with the perspective, "God, all of this is Yours. I can't be destroyed by what You pour into and through my life because I'm a river, not a pond. *What You pour into my hands will actually pour 'on through' me at Your direction for Your purposes.*"

Recall how Jesus said it in Matthew 6:19-20 NIV.

> [19] *"Do not store up for yourselves treasures on earth, where moths and vermin destroy, and where thieves break in and steal.* [20] *But store up for yourselves treasures in heaven, where moths and vermin do not destroy, and where thieves do not break in and steal."*

Here's a paraphrase of that passage:

"I want to pour more into and through you than you could ever imagine. But *don't store up for yourselves on earth* what I pour into your hands. When you let what I pour <u>*into*</u> your hands <u>*flow on through*</u> you at My direction and for My purposes, in a way you cannot understand (yet), *you are actually storing up treasures for yourself in eternity.*"

In other words, God is telling us, "Don't store up for yourselves stuff here on Earth. It won't fulfill you to begin with. It creates more drag for you to manage. If you just hang onto it, it will become a distraction and it will ultimately destroy you. When I pour it in, let it pour on through. I'll make sure that your needs are met. *I'll make sure you have enough coming in to meet your needs but not your greeds (all our wants)."*

That may sound a little harsh. But most of the time, "lifestyle" choices ("new" this, "new" that, "latest" the other...) are what strain people's finances.

* *

I'll never forget the first time I heard a Biblical finance teacher make the point, *"If you can't make it on 90% of your income, you won't make it on 100% either. Because the problem isn't the amount of the income. It's the lack of submitting your desires under God's guidance. You're choosing to buy things that either He wouldn't say yes to (or say yes to yet.) When you choose to commit to something that God didn't guide you to do, He's not on the hook to sustain it either."* Ouch!! That stung me just a little...

REFLECTION QUESTIONS

1. *Reflect on the concept that God calls His tithe a "unique something" that is part of everything that is already His. How does recognizing the holiness of the tithe influence your understanding of its significance in your relationship with God?*
2. *Explore the distinction between "giving" and "bringing" the tithe, as mentioned in this chapter. How does this shift in language impact your perception of the tithe, and what practical implications does it have for your approach to tithing?*
3. *Reflect on the idea that the tithe is described as the redemptive portion and parallels the sacrifice and redemption principles seen in the Bible. How does this understanding deepen your appreciation for the significance of the tithe in the context of God's love and our redemption through Jesus Christ?*
4. *Contemplate the principle of "storing up treasures in heaven" by allowing what God pours into your life to flow through you for His purposes. How does this perspective challenge common cultural views on accumulating wealth and possessions?*

CHAPTER 7: LIVING UNDER A CURSE?

In the previous chapters, we have seen how God designed a way for us to align the desires of our heart with Him and His Kingdom by returning the holy portion - His tithe - to His house as worship. We have also seen how some people choose to do other things with His tithe (either through ignorance or by rejecting His direction). Here is how God describes the results of that choice.

> [8] *"Will a mere mortal rob God? Yet you rob me. But you ask, 'How are we robbing you?'" "In tithes and offerings.* [9] *You are under a curse — your whole nation — because you are robbing me."*
> *Malachi 3:8-9 NIV*

What were they robbing Him of? Money? Let's take this apart and look at it.

God said they were robbing Him in tithes and offerings. As a result, they were living under a curse. Many times, the tithe message feels like it's being leveraged over us because if we don't tithe, then God will curse us. That is not what God is saying at all.

What He said was, "You <u>are</u> under a curse." He did NOT say, "I have cursed you." He says, "You are living under a curse. You are operating your lives by the ways and values of a system or kingdom that is not Mine. As such, I can't bless you the way I want to."

Why not? Because they would ultimately "consume" the limitless blessings of God on their own desires <u>**which would destroy them**</u>.

When we don't return His tithe and then do what He says to do with the offering, we are basically saying, "God, regardless of what You say, You do not have my heart (trust and commitment)."

So, what's He really searching for? It's not our money, it's our heart. Jesus, again answers that question in Matthew 6:21 NIV.

> [21] *"Wherever your treasure is, there the desires of your heart will also be."*

In large part, "our heart desiring Him" is what He is looking for with this whole expression of tithing.

So, Malachi 3:8-9 outlines the <u>**problem**</u> God wants them to recognize. Then He outlines the <u>**solution**</u> in Malachi 3:10 NIV.

> [10] *"Bring the whole tithe into the storehouse, that there may be food in my house. Test me in this," says the LORD*

> Almighty, *"and see if I will not throw open the floodgates of heaven and pour out so much blessing that there will not be room enough to store it."*

Stop! Before you throw in the towel and write this whole idea off as being limited to Old Testament <u>Law</u>, think that through. The practice of tithing is far older than the Old Testament Law.

The practice of tithing was demonstrated <u>*long before*</u> God gave His people the law. It is a <u>***pre-law***</u> function of response from the heart of humans whose desires were after God. Tithing was an instinctive response. And it actually first shows up in God's Bible in the very first book. Genesis 4:3-5a NKJV says:

> [3] *And in the process of time it came to pass that Cain brought an offering of the fruit of the ground to the LORD.* [4] *Abel also brought of the firstborn of his flock and of their fat. And the LORD respected Abel and his offering,* [5] *but He did not respect Cain and his offering.*

The account of Cain and his brother, Abel, eventually reaches its tragic end - Cain murders Abel. But from verses 3-5, we see that Cain basically was going about His harvest doing whatever He wanted to do, and <u>in the process of time, he decided</u>, "Well, I'm going to take some to God, too."

Abel, however, actually recognized, "This all belongs to God, and I'm taking Him my first and finest to Him as worship."

God also shows us tithing in Genesis through Abraham and Jacob as well, so it is recorded as a worship practice early in the Old Testament. It's referenced in the Old Testament law, but it wasn't *initiated* by the law. Tithing was part of mankind's original relational connection with God.

In the New Testament, we catch up with Jesus as He was correcting some of the religious leaders (Pharisees).

> [23] *"What sorrow awaits you teachers of religious law and you Pharisees. Hypocrites! For you are careful to tithe even the tiniest income from your herb gardens, but you ignore the more important aspects of the law — justice, mercy, and faith. You should tithe, yes, but do not neglect the more important things."*
>
> *Matthew 23:23 NLT*

Jesus was saying to them, "I see you bringing the tithe. But the tithe isn't the most important thing. You are flashing your tithing around and saying, 'Look, I even tithe on the mint and herbs in my hands.' Jesus said, "You got that one down and you should be doing that. But **what you're leaving out** (justice, mercy and faith) is actually more important." Jesus was basically saying, "Tithing is just the floor. It isn't the big stuff."

People that appeal to Jesus in the New Testament *to get out of tithing* are actually painting themselves into a pretty tight corner. Jesus took everything that is a moral imperative or a hard application in the Old Testament and ramped it up in the New Testament.

So, God says in the Old Testament, "An eye for an eye." In the New Testament, "Love Your enemy."

In the Old Testament, "Don't murder." In the New Testament, "Don't speak harshly against a brother."

In the Old Testament, "Do not commit adultery." In the New Testament, "If you lust after a woman, you've committed adultery in Your heart."

Here's what's going on. God is basically **not** saying, "I just want your behavior to be correct." He's saying, "I want your heart, I want you, and here's how I designed life in relationship with Me to work."

Refusing to return God's tithe is a relational disconnect that robs Him of something He wants to do in, for and through us.

<u>So what does living under a curse look like</u>? We have a perfect picture of what that curse looks like in Haggai 1:5-6 NLT.

> *⁵ This is what the LORD of Heaven's Armies says: "Look at what's happening to you! ⁶ You have planted much but harvest little. You eat but are not satisfied. You drink but are still thirsty. You put on clothes but cannot keep warm. Your wages disappear as*

though you were putting them in pockets filled with holes!"

That is what living under a curse looks like. It's like we're going through the motions of what ought to work, but for reasons that aren't obvious, it isn't working.

It's like the increase coming into our hands is being devoured before it becomes fulfilling.

REFLECTION QUESTIONS

1. *Reflect on the idea that living under a curse, as mentioned in Malachi, is not a direct curse from God but rather a consequence of aligning with values and systems that are not in line with His Kingdom. How does this understanding shift your perspective on blessings and curses?*
2. *Explore the concept that tithing is not solely a legalistic obligation but a response from the heart, as demonstrated by examples like Cain and Abel in Genesis. How does this perspective change the way you view the practice of tithing?*
3. *Examine the description of living under a curse in Haggai 1:5-6. How does this imagery resonate with your understanding of the challenges and dissatisfaction that may arise when financial resources are not aligned with God's design, including the practice of tithing?*

CHAPTER 8: LIVING UNDER GOD'S LIMITLESS BLESSING

What does God say to do in order to plug the holes of living under a curse? He says in Malachi 3:10 NIV,

> [10] *"Bring the whole tithe into the storehouse, that there may be food in my house. Test me in this," says the LORD Almighty, "and see if I will not throw open the floodgates of heaven and pour out so much blessing that there will not be room enough to store it."*

There is a chance that Malachi 3:10 is so familiar, you just skipped over it and thought, "Yeah, I got it." **But God is actually telling us something that we need to truly know - and do**.

Maybe you didn't skip over that verse. But for the benefit of those who did, let's actually re-read it - this time with emphasis.

> [10] ***"Bring the whole tithe into the storehouse, that there may be food in my***

> *house. Test me in this," says the LORD Almighty, "and see if I will not throw open the floodgates of heaven and pour out so much blessing that there will not be room enough to store it."*
>
> Malachi 3:10 NIV

What God tells **us** to do:

- Bring God's whole (holy) tithe into the storehouse (your local church).

What God tells us **He** will do:

- Throw open the floodgates of heaven…
- Pour out so much blessing…

Okay, so God stated that He will carry out two different functions.

1. First is the opening of the floodgates.
2. There is also a second function - the pouring out of His blessing.

** Notice: **Just because the floodgates are open doesn't mean the pouring is happening. The floodgates can be open -** *with no pouring happening.*

I want to point out that, when God said in Malachi 3:8, "Will a mere mortal rob God? Yet you rob me, but you ask, 'How are we robbing you?' In tithes and offerings."

Notice God said they were robbing Him of <u>tithes</u> **and** <u>offerings</u>.

The **tithe** is *God's holy part*. He instructs us to return that to Him through our local church.

The **offering** is a *separate (and distinctly different) response* to God's subsequent leading.

God clearly points out that when we refuse to collaborate and participate with Him in returning His tithe <u>and</u> giving offerings as He directs, *it robs Him of something He wants to do in, for and through us*.

I want to encourage you to see that **returning His tithe** is what allows God to <u>open the floodgates</u>.

It's **the offering** that <u>facilitates His pouring out</u>.

Let's read that again and carefully notice what God said He would pour out:

> [10] *"Bring the whole tithe into the storehouse, that there may be food in my house. Test me in this," says the LORD Almighty, "and see if I will not throw open the floodgates of heaven and pour out so much blessing that there will not be room enough to store it."*
>
> *Malachi 3:10 NIV*

One more time. "...And see if I will not throw open the flood gates of heaven and pour out so much blessing that there will not be room enough to..." *What?* To <u>**store**</u> it.

God is saying, "The blessing I want to pour out is **_THE UNSTORABLE BLESSING_**."

God is definitely not into hoarding wealth for the sake of "having" it. He does, however, make it clear in His Bible that He directs His people to steward wealth in varying degrees to accomplish His purposes (see examples in parables Jesus used in Matthew 25:14-30 and Luke 19:11-27 to teach this principle).

Since He wants His people to steward wealth as part of His shaping process in their lives, He also has a process of providing it for them to use. Here are two (of several) different ways God moves the blessing of wealth into the lives of His people.

1. **God gives His people the _ability to produce_ wealth.**

   > [18] *But remember the LORD your God, for it is he who gives you the ability to produce wealth, and so confirms his covenant, which he swore to your ancestors, as it is today*
   >
   > Deuteronomy 8:18 NIV

2. **There is wealth _stored up_ for the use of His people to accomplish His purposes.**

   > [22] *... But the wealth of the sinner is stored up for the righteous.*
   >
   > Proverbs 13:22b NKJV

These two ways are the *"production" of new wealth* and the *"transfer" of stored up wealth*.

Through either way, or a combination of both ways, **God has the power to pour _unstorable blessing_ (limitless wealth) into the lives of His people**.

To summarize:

- **First: Returning God's holy tithe to Him through His storehouse (our local church) _enables Him to "open the floodgates" of heaven over our lives_.**
  - Note: Remember that Jesus said in Matthew 6:21, "The "desires of our heart" follows our treasure" and that God tells us in Hebrews 7:8 that, "When we return His holy tithe here on earth, He receives them in heaven."
  - With that in mind, another way of picturing that is to say that returning God's holy tithe to Him through His storehouse (our local church) effectively puts the "desires of our heart" into "His hands".
  - With the power of our desires placed firmly in God's hands, He can open the floodgates (protective barriers) of heaven that previously protected us from being flooded with His infinite blessings.
  - Why would He "protect" us from that scale of His blessings?
  - _Before_ our hearts' desires were for Him (in His hands), they would have led us to consume

every blessing that came into our lives upon our own selfish desires - ultimately destroying our lives.
- **Then: Giving offerings as God directs us to, gives Him the ability then to pour out the "<u>unstorable blessing</u>"** (more on this blessing later in the book).

So, Malachi 3:10 ends with the phrase, "*pour out so much blessing that there will not be room enough to* **store** *it.*"

Next, God describes His divine intervention in response to their obedience with returning His tithe and giving offerings.

> [11] *"I will prevent pests from devouring your crops, and the vines in your fields will not drop their fruit before it is ripe," says the LORD Almighty.*
> *Malachi 3:11 NIV*

Finally, God highlights the end result of this process (they'll live in a delightful land). The contrast between God's people and other lands will be so substantial that people will be compelled to acknowledge God and His divine favor on their lives (all nations will call you blessed).

> [12] *"Then all the nations will call you blessed, for yours will be a delightful land," says the LORD Almighty.*
> *Malachi 3:12 NIV*

That scripture gives us some insight into why God wants this element in our lives so intentionally. There is something that happens when people collaborate with God in the way He directs them to. Doing so gives Him the ability to create something obvious <u>through their obedience that demonstrates who He is</u>. "Nations will call you blessed." Why will they call us blessed? Because the evidence of God's blessing overwhelms our reality.

Part of discipling nations is flowing in the supernatural blessings of God that causes people to look at what is happening and say, "You are blessed." In other words, "I want what you have. How do I get that?" And you say, "Well, let me introduce you to the Blesser."

Here's one more dimension of what is happening when we return God's tithe to the storehouse (our local church).

Hebrews 7:8 is one of the most insightful verses in the scripture. *It is a parallel to something Jesus illustrated when He was explaining another principle in how His Kingdom works* in Matthew 25:34-40 NLT:

> [34] *Then the King will say to those on his right, "Come, you who are blessed by my Father, inherit the Kingdom prepared for you from the creation of the world.* [35] *For **I** was hungry, and <u>you fed **me**</u>. **I** was thirsty, and <u>you gave **me** a drink</u>. **I** was a stranger, and <u>you invited **me** into your home</u>.* [36] ***I** was naked, and <u>you gave **me** clothing</u>.*

*I was sick, and you cared for **me**. I was in prison, and you visited **me**.*"

³⁷ *Then these righteous ones will reply, "Lord, when did we ever see you hungry and feed you? Or thirsty and give you something to drink?* ³⁸ *Or a stranger and show you hospitality? Or naked and give you clothing?* ³⁹ *When did we ever see you sick or in prison and visit you?"*

⁴⁰ *And the King will say, "I tell you the truth, when you did it to one of the least of these my brothers and sisters, you were doing it to **me**!*" (author's emphasis)

He's basically saying, "There are things that you do that are not just for the person you're doing them to. In a way that you don't understand, **you are actually doing that to Me at the same time**."

You may be wondering how this relates to returning God's tithe and giving offerings as He directs from what is "in our hands." Here is how.

In Hebrews, God shows us a clear picture of what is happening there in heaven as we return His tithe here on earth.

> [8] *Here (on earth) mortal men receive tithes, but there (in heaven) he (Jesus) receives them, of whom it is witnessed that he lives.*
> *Hebrews 7:8 NKJV*

What's he saying?

When we return God's tithe to Him at our local church, humans will "handle" it. A human is going to count it. A human is going to put it in the bank. A human is going to enter that contribution in the data collection system, etc.

God is saying, "There on earth, humans received My tithe. But don't think that's what it's about. *I don't need that treasure.* <u>*I gave you that directive in order to give you a way to steer the desires of your heart towards Me. In a way you don't see, I actually do receive that tithe in Heaven.*</u> **But what you are actually doing is putting your heart in My hands**."

Ultimately, everything comes down to where our heart is, and we want our hearts in His hands. So, we joyfully take the tithe and return it to the storehouse (our local church) here on earth - *which translates to Him receiving it in heaven.* People who "understand this" realize returning God's tithe as He outlines in His Bible is not simply "paying a religious tax." Instead, they live out the reality that of treasuring God and His Kingdom more than anything on this earth.

REFLECTION QUESTIONS

1. *Reflect on the concept that returning the tithe allows God to open the floodgates, while giving offerings facilitates the pouring out of unstorable blessings. How can you apply this understanding in your own financial stewardship?*
2. *Explore the idea that the act of returning God's tithe is not just a practical financial transaction on earth but has a significant spiritual dimension in heaven. How does this perspective influence your motivation for tithing?*
3. *Consider the broader impact of living under God's blessing, as described in Malachi 3:11-12. How does obedience in returning the tithe and giving offerings contribute to a life that attracts others to acknowledge God's favor and blessing?*

CHAPTER 9: THE DIFFERENCE BETWEEN SEEDS AND BREAD

God defines how He "measures harvest (increase) back into our lives" and "the purposes He accomplishes through our generosity" in a process outlined in 2 Corinthians 9:6-8 NIV.

> *⁶ Remember this: Whoever sows sparingly will also reap sparingly, and whoever sows generously will also reap generously.*

- The reaping ratio is tied to the sowing ratio.
- Next we'll see that sowing is identified as giving.

> *⁷ Each of you should give what you have decided in your heart to give, not reluctantly or under compulsion, for God loves a cheerful giver.*

- God is saying, "I want you to <u>decide in your heart</u> to give <u>what I lead you to give</u>. I never want you to

- give based on someone making you feel manipulated or guilt-tripped into giving."
- Why? Because reluctant or compelled giving is giving something away that you are attached to. It feels like giving something away that was yours and important to you. That's not cheerfully giving.
- Cheerful giving is when we give <u>with no sense of loss</u>.

> *⁸ And God is able to bless you abundantly, so that in all things at all times, having all that you need, you will abound in every good work."*

- God is <u>able</u>. We tend to think, "Well of course He's able. He's God, He can do *anything*."

When we recall the insight God shows us in Haggai 1:6 (eat but not satisfied, drink but still thirsty, work wages disappear...) we realize that <u>there are limits to what He's willing to do</u> - <u>but the limit is not on His side</u>. (Those limits are actually love on His part). <u>The limit is from our side</u>.

Remember 2 Chronicles 16:9a NIV:

> *⁹ For the eyes of the LORD (search) throughout the earth to strengthen (show himself faithful to) those whose hearts are fully committed to him.*

In other words, God is looking for someone who is willing to say "yes'"to whatever He puts their hands.

Why? **Because that's what gives Him the ability to pour limitless - unstorable - resources through their lives constructively**.

Notice the two different types of resources God provides in 2 Corinthians 9:10-15 NIV.

> *¹⁰ Now he who supplies seed to the sower and bread for food will also supply and increase your store of seed and will enlarge the harvest of your righteousness.*

- <u>Seed to the sower</u> is **not the same** as <u>bread for food</u>.
- Bread for food refers to processed, ready-to-eat bread (solutions) for immediate needs to be met.
- God intends for us to "eat" (consume) what He supplies as "bread for food" (resources for what we need to operate with).
- **But He provides "seed" for a different purpose: <u>Sowing (giving)</u>.**
- Sowing (giving) generously as God leads, gives Him the ability to bring an even larger harvest back into our stewardship.
- If we "eat" the "seed," we won't "get the harvest." God wants to supply through our sowing. But we won't "get a harvest" from the seed we eat.

- Notice God's **intent** in the increasing harvest in our lives:

¹¹ You will be enriched in every way so that you can be generous on every occasion, and through us your generosity will result in thanksgiving to God.

- The whole process ultimately results in God getting glory.
- Notice the multiple uses being accomplished by our collaboration with God through giving generously:

¹² This service that you perform is not only supplying the needs of the Lord's people but is also overflowing in many expressions of thanks to God.

- The "seed" we sow becomes the "supply" for others' needs AND;
- Causes people to give thanks to God for "His provision."

¹³ Because of the service by which you have proved yourselves, others will praise God for the obedience that accompanies your confession of the gospel of Christ, and for your generosity in sharing with them and with everyone else.

- Following God's leadership in giving generously is evidence of our personal growth AND;
- It becomes part of our "sharing the Gospel of Christ."

¹⁴ And in their prayers for you their hearts will go out to you, because of the surpassing grace God has given you.

- Obedience in this function inspires people to pray for and think well of us, because of God's clear work through us.

¹⁵ Thanks be to God for his indescribable gift!
2 Corinthians 8:10-15 NIV

The vast majority of the time, when God wants to meet a need, He does so by providing a seed for someone else to sow, which becomes a harvest that both meets that need and provides additional seed to be sown for the next harvest.

Seed is the only thing with potential to increase or multiply. Once it's bread, it's dead.

REFLECTION QUESTIONS

1. *How does the principle of sowing and reaping, as outlined in 2 Corinthians 9:6-8, influence your understanding of generosity and the abundance of blessings in your life?*
2. *Reflect on the distinction between "bread for food" and "seed to the sower." How can you ensure that you are appropriately using the resources provided by God for immediate needs and for sowing generously?*
3. *Consider the multiple purposes and outcomes of generous giving outlined in 2 Corinthians 9:11-15. How does your generosity contribute not only to meeting immediate needs but also to sharing the Gospel and inspiring gratitude and praise to God?*
4. *How can the concept that "seed is the only thing with the potential to increase or multiply" impact your perspective on the resources in your life? How might this understanding influence your choices in using and giving what God provides?*

CHAPTER 10: HOW TO RECEIVE THE UNSTORABLE BLESSING

Gotcha! You definitely did it – saw the chapter title in the Table of Contents and turned <u>straight</u> to this chapter. Do yourself a life-changing favor. STOP RIGHT HERE, go back to the Introduction (or even the Foreword) and start from the beginning. Why? There is a near 100% chance you will <u>completely miss</u> the layers of developmental insights that actually bring this chapter to life. For real – go back and take the eye-opening journey through this short book. Before you know it, you'll be right back here but ready for it this time.

No, really – you'll thank me for the shove...

* *

Can you imagine reaching the place in your relationship with God that He would intrust unimaginable - unstorable - resources into your stewardship on His behalf? God can imagine you there. Why? Because you were made for that!

Let's boil this process down to six simple (but maybe not initially easy) steps.

SIX STEPS THAT RELEASE GOD TO POUR HIS UNSTORABLE BLESSINGS INTO OUR LIVES:

1. **We remind ourselves that everything belongs to God (Psalm 24:1). No "thing" or "nothing" but God can truly fill or fulfill us.**

No tangible or material stuff can do that. No status can do it. No experience can do it. God is the only one that can truly fulfill us. He owns it all (and puts some of it into our hands to manage on His behalf).

2. **We decide to live and function in His kingdom.**

How? The first thing to do is remember that He owns it all, *but a portion of what is already His, He also says is holy*. He calls it His tithe. He says, "Return it to my storehouse (your local church)" (Malachi 3:10)

So even if we don't understand how all of it works, we return the first 10% of all of our increase "to" God "through" our local church (Hebrews 7:8 NKJV)

Some people ask, "Do I tithe on the gross or the net?" We generate the gross so we should return God's tithe of the gross we generated.

3. **We *prayerfully* set (and operate from) a budget that has margin for generosity built into it**

(which restrains us from consuming everything that comes into our hands).

<u>Here's where many people miss the bus</u>. This is the actual, rubber-meets-the-road stuff...

We work with God's guidance to develop a functional annual and monthly budget that truly covers our essentials (including tithing, savings - short and long-term, housing, transportation, additional lifestyle-related things – AND MARGIN FOR GENEROSITY)

- **If we return God's tithe first, <u>then spend everything else</u>, we still have a problem.**

What problem? <u>No margin for generosity</u>. When we return His 10% and then spend the other 90% on "what we want," there is no "seed left to sow."

God is looking for people to move massive amounts of resources "through." But many people feel like they've "done their part" and "God should be happy enough" with their tithe. They hardly have "enough left to get what they **want**" after that...

There it is again - THE WANTER!

The only way to keep our wanter from totally consuming our lives is to put a real limit on it. (Remember, there is no "satisfying" it anyway...) If we don't put an external limit on our wanter, we will eat everything that comes into our hands, <u>including the seed</u>. Why?

Because it looks just like everything else that came into our hands to meet our needs (and "wanters have needs, too...").

The best way to determine that with God ahead of time, is to prayerfully say, "God, this year, how much do I budget for the different categories of my life?" And He'll tell you, "Return My tithe first. Then designate X% for this category, designate X% for that category, designate X% for this category and designate X% for generosity, etc."

That budget should cover our needs. It should reflect God's wisdom of savings. And it should still have margin in it to allow us to joyfully give as God directs.

You may be thinking, "Okay. This is solid thinking - *but nothing really insightful yet*. Get ready. *The next step is what may open a completely new level of possibilities to collaborate with God*.

4. **We set aside everything that comes in above that budget as what God provided as "seed to sow."**

At this point, a common reaction comes across like, "No way! I just got a raise." Or, "I couldn't do that! I've been waiting a long time to get..."

The mindset that makes this step possible is one of "Godliness with contentment." Remember how God frames this reality in 1 Timothy 6.

> [6] *But godliness with contentment is great gain.* [7] *For we brought nothing into the*

> *world, and we can take nothing out of it. ⁸ But if we have food and clothing, we will be content with that. ⁹ Those who want to get rich fall into temptation and a trap and into many foolish and harmful desires that plunge people into ruin and destruction. ¹⁰ For the love of money is a root of all kinds of evil. Some people, eager for money, have wandered from the faith and pierced themselves with many griefs.*
>
> 1 Timothy 6:6-10 NIV

In other words, since God lets us know that great gain is not accomplished by getting more great stuff, we're free to let Him guide us with a budget for each year that provides everything we actually need. That budget would cover returning His tithe, meeting the needs of our household, savings (short and long term), and margin to cover joyful giving and generosity.

Then, when unplanned resources come into our stewardship, they are obvious to us, which releases us to actually let them flow right "through us" to wherever God guides us to give them.

God's wisdom about savings is real. It's hoarding that's not wise. So we budget for His tithe, for savings, for our needs, for generosity and then whatever comes in above that, set it aside to give where God guides. Why?

Because that's our way of saying, "God, here's the container that I won't eat from. Dump anything you want in it and I'll carry it to the need."

This will not work without a budget. Why? Because a budget is actually a vision. Habakkuk 2 is where God tells us to write the vision and make it plain so we can run the vision.

Once we have a budget (vision) that covers us for the year, then we're set. And we can freely respond with a million dollar windfall that shows up because a long-lost uncle passed away who had a gold mine somewhere. When that happens, we'd be able to say, *"Well, that million dollars is way bigger than what God worked out with me for this year's budget. So that must mean God wants to actually move those funds through me. Okay, God, You can move that million through me like that. Where do You want me to give it?"*

Maybe the thought is, "Are you kidding me right now?" <u>If so, that's why you haven't experienced this yet</u>.

Once we get our "unsubmitted desires" submitted under God's vision, He is free to pour "Unstorable Blessings" into and through our lives.

5. **We sow (give) all the seed from step 4 as God directs us to.**

Whatever comes into that "over and above" bucket, that is "seed to sow," we give away as God shows us where He wants it.

6. **We repeat the same vision (budget) process with God every year (and get ready to see more**

and more seed come into our hands to sow on His behalf).

In other words, once we get through a year this way, God says, "Man, I have found a servant I can move money through!" Then we say, "God, let's talk about next year." And He says, "I want you to budget for a hundred thousand dollars _more_ in your annual household vision budget because I know I can do more through you. So create a bigger vision budget for next year. Make sure it's got margin for generosity, savings, household needs like I'm showing you, and then give me the 'over and above' container and I'll put more seed money into that one that you can sow where I show you to."

Perhaps within two or three years of collaborating with God like this, we may find ourselves in the same position as R. G. Letourneau. From humble beginnings, he rose - in "partnership with God" - to extraordinary wealth and ultimately lived on 10% and gave 90% of his earnings away (see article below).

"He was a kind man, a man who many said had a slide ruler in one hand and a Bible in the other. He was a common man, a self-educated man that rose to the top of the earthmoving business. His business—and his life—was guided by one principle, which he was happy to tell every writer that ever did a story on him. "God runs my business," he would say, a big smile breaking out on his friendly face.

- *Throughout his life, R.G. LeTourneau was awarded more than 300 patents for his innovations in earthmoving equipment, manufacturing processes and machine tools.*
- *LeTourneau supplied between 50 and 70 percent of all the earthmoving equipment used by the Allies during World War II.*
- *LeTourneau pioneered the development of pre-fabricated, steel-welded homes, primarily to furnish housing for his employees. More than 20 went up near the plant in Peoria, while others were floated up and down the Illinois River to their locations.*
- *LeTourneau also developed the first portable offshore drilling platform in the mid-1950s.*

Throughout his life he was referred to as "God's Businessman." In a blink of his friendly eye, he would quote the book of Matthew, verse 33: "But seek ye first the Kingdom Of God, and his righteousness, and all these things will be added unto you." That's who R.G. really was.

Born in Vermont, Virginia, on November 30, 1888, he would accumulate over 300 patents in the course of his lifetime.

By 1911, he was a partner in an auto repair shop, and soon became an expert mechanic, with a total understanding of the combustion engine. He married Evelyn Peterson in 1917, and together they reared three boys and a girl.

In 1920 he bought a used Holt tractor and began a grading business. In late 1921, he had his own machine shop where he designed and built different types of scrapers and electrical engines. Soon after that, he formed the R.G. LeTourneau Company that would bring him fame and riches beyond even his imaginative dreams.

His company was involved in massive projects like the Hoover Dam, and numerous road-building contracts that kept him busy until 1933. Unable to devote enough of his time to his inventing and dreams of manufacturing his own machines, he sold the business. It was 1935, when R.G. came to Peoria with the idea of building his factory and getting on with his dream. From that day forward, the rest is history, as folks like to say, and most of his dreams came true right here.

So for R.G., it all started in a small brick building on the north side of Peoria, Illinois. His inventive mind and hard-working ethics would take him all over the world, amassing a fortune as he went. In 1953, he sold the Peoria business to Westinghouse Air Brake Company (WABCO) for a cool $25 million. **Biographers of R.G. LeTourneau pretty much agree that he donated 90 percent of his fortune to charities and Christian organizations**."

https://www.peoriamagazine.com/archive/ibi_article/2011/rg-letourneau/

REFLECTION QUESTIONS

1. *How does the concept of acknowledging that everything belongs to God, including our resources, influence your perspective on stewardship and generosity?*
2. *How do you currently approach budgeting, and in what ways can you integrate a mindset of generosity and margin for giving into your financial planning?*
3. *What challenges do you foresee in setting aside resources above your budget as "seed to sow," and how can you cultivate a mindset of contentment to enable this step?*
4. *Reflect on the idea of collaborating with God in financial planning. How might incorporating God's guidance into your budget create a vision that allows for both wise stewardship and joyful giving?*

CONCLUSION

Thank you for taking the time to read through this book. My prayer for you is that God has opened your thinking to a way of handling finances in a manner that lets Him pour, by orders of magnitude, **more resources into and through your yes than you can even imagine** (Ephesians 3:20).

- **He is looking for people like that** (2 Chron. 16:9) **and,**
- **You were made for His supernatural purposes** (Ephesians 2:10).

I believe that God will do the same for you as He has done for us - take the process outlined in this book and <u>turn your **yes** in this area of giving into an alignment with Him and His Kingdom that frees you from limiting thought patterns and transforms the way finances work in your life</u>.

I invite you to put the six practical steps outlined in Chapter 10 into practice and be prepared for God to expand your territory in profound ways.

We love hearing stories of people who have experienced this blessing in their lives. We would love to hear your story as well. Please feel free to share your story, be inspired by stories like yours and synergize with other people whose lives are a pathway for God's Unstorable Blessing. You can connect with additional resources and a community of givers through this website: *__theunstorableblessing.com__*

May God's immeasurable presence, power and blessing overwhelm you on your journey.

David Wright

Proverbs 4:23

ABOUT THE AUTHOR

Since 1989, David Wright has been happily married to his incredible wife, Chereé. Together, they take pride in their roles as parents to two daughters, Lacie and Tori, as well as Son-In-Law James and two precious granddaughters, Emma and Nova. In 2006, they started and together co-lead Life Link Church in the SE Phoenix Valley (lifelinkchurch.com). David, a gifted teacher, is dedicated to empowering individuals to lead meaningful and impactful lives, drawing strength from the profound power of God's Word and Spirit.

theunstorableblessing.com

Made in the USA
Las Vegas, NV
22 October 2024